Chapter One – In the Beginning

Picture this. You walk up to the counter at your local pharmacy. You tell the person your name and they scramble around eventually telling you that your prescription isn't ready. How many of you have had this happen to you? I want you to start to think of the things that go through your mind. I will guess a few:

1) "They have 6 people back there. How the heck is it not ready?"
2) "The doctor said my prescription would be ready when I got here."

3) "The pharmacist is just standing there typing and ignoring me."

4) "That pharmacist is just standing there on the phone not doing anything."

5) "All they have to do it slap a label on the box and hand it to me."

6) "This pharmacy is terrible. I wish my insurance would allow me to go to a different one."

And if your prescription is ready and you don't like the price, you think "Did this go up again?"

Well let me tell you, while your thoughts are valid, the fact is, there is way more to it than all of this. I am going to use this book as a means to tell you about the underworld of pharmacy. Basically, you will learn the innerworkings and what's in place in your local pharmacy that make the quick trip near impossible. Before you go off thinking that this person doesn't know what he's talking about, let me give you a little information about myself.

It all started in my high school English class. I had the same English teacher for three straight years. For those of you thinking, did he fail English? The answer is no. In my high school, certain teachers would teach the progression of the class (i.e. English I, English II, etc). Every year before Christmas, we would watch *It's a Wonderful Life* in this class. I saw George Bailey work for Mr. Gower and it clicked. From that point forward I knew I wanted to be a pharmacist. I started working at a major chain pharmacy in the late 1990s. I worked with two amazing pharmacists who taught me about forming connections with patients. One actually owned her own independent pharmacy before being bought out by one of the major chains. I eventually went on to pharmacy school in Pennsylvania graduating in 2006. During my years in pharmacy school, I did school educational rotations in hospital administration, mail order pharmacy, compounding pharmacy, as well as independent pharmacies. Upon graduation, I became licensed in three different states. I started my career as a staff pharmacist ultimately being promoted to pharmacy manager in less than a year.

During the early years of my pharmacist career, my supervisor always told me to treat my pharmacy like my own independent. I took this advice and flourished eventually becoming pharmacy managers of various locations. It was during this time as a manager that I learned how evil pharmacy truly was. It eventually caused me to leave the company I had been with for 20+ years and take a job as a staff pharmacist at another major chain pharmacy. Let me tell you, once you see this evil, there is no unseeing it.

Chapter Two – How It Was

When I started in the late 90s, pharmacy was a great landscape. Pharmacies were pharmacies. Insurance companies were insurance companies. Most importantly, Pharmacy Benefits Managers (PBMs) did not have major control over things. I will tell you that if you don't know what a PBM is, I strongly suggest you do a deep dive into what they are, how they work, and what they do to impact your life. I will take some time later on to give an overview on them, but this is a rabbit hole you really should go down if you are to better understand why your copays keep escalating and why prior authorizations are becoming the norm as well as many other things that frustrate you thinking it is the pharmacist's fault.

Back to the lovely late 90s. When you went to the doctor wearing your platform boots listening to *Alice in Chains*, you would see your actual doctor who took his or her time with you. This doctor most likely knew your entire family. They had been seeing you, your parents, and your siblings. You would eventually be given a paper prescription with some scribbles on it. You took these hieroglyphics to the local pharmacy, handed to a smiling technician who most likely knew your name as well as all of your family's names and started typing away. They would slap a sticker on that paper prescription and hand it to the pharmacist. Assuming the internet was working correctly and the pharmacy computer system was up and running properly and with the pharmacist's verification, a prescription label would be printed. The label would be used to find the correct medication bottle off the shelf to be used to count your specific prescription. Meanwhile, the multiple other technicians would be answering the phone taking refill prescription numbers to add to the ever-mounting number of prescriptions to fill or attempting to fill those very prescriptions. Once the little basket of pills was verified by the pharmacist, it would be stapled together and handed to someone to ring you out at the register. For the most part, this process was followed by smiling pharmacy team members. This was before the dark times, before the PBM and Drug Company empires.

Chapter Three – Pharmacy Benefits Managers (PBMs)

As stated earlier, these PBMs are pure evil. They provide window dressing letting you think they actually are doing good, but the fact is, they are a major cause of the ever-increasing prescription drug prices. I urge you to read about the full history of PBMs as well as what they do but will summarize it for you. The first PBM was founded in 1968. In the beginning times, they would be the go between processing prescription paper claims until technological advancements converted that to electronic claims. There were multiple players in this process, but as time went on, as it does with all businesses, consolidation occurred. Bigger companies who focused on specific parts of the process would buy out a smaller company who focused on something completely different. As this consolidation occurred, the dreaded PBM was born. On the surface, the PBMs sold themselves as heroes as they moved doctors towards prescribing cheaper generic medication alternatives. On the back side, they were sneakily marketing the more expensive brand name medications out there.

In 2007 the landscape drastically changed. CVS, a well-known pharmacy purchased Caremark, a well known PBM as well as insurance company. It was at this time the PBM spiral began. No longer were PBMs just adjudicating prescriptions, they were now being the managers of their employees' pharmacy benefits. This may not mean much to you, however it was at this point where your local pharmacist's job drastically changed. They were no longer "just filling prescriptions." They were now providing disease state management, medication compliance, as well as drug utilization reviews (DURs) and vaccination cold calls.

Let me be clear, I am not downplaying these other jobs, however the expectation of the pharmacy chains has created quite the dynamic for your local pharmacist. More on that later. As PBMs progressed, formularies began. I'm sure you've heard of them. Comments from your pharmacist such as "this isn't on your formulary, it's a Tier 2 medication, or it requires a prior authorization" have been told to you. Don't blame your pharmacist, blame your PBM. As a fun statistic and as of the writing of this, the three biggest PBMs; CVS/Health, Express Scripts, and United Health control roughly 81% of the market. Let's flash back to your economics class. When there are very few options out there, what can the supplier do? If you answered, they can create pretty much any price they want and set the market, you are correct. What is unique about this, however, is that demand is being inflated as well. What do I mean? If you look at the rates of medications being prescribed annually, you will see the number in the 4 billions and increasing each year. If you take a snapshot of 2022 alone in the United States, it means that each person living in the United States is prescribed approximately 15 prescriptions per year!!! And these numbers are only going up.

    The kicker of this is that since these PBMs run the insurance portion as well as a pharmacy portion, there is no telling what backdoor deals are occurring at the expense of the United States citizen. Think about it. Who audits these pharmacies? I mean, who oversees that they aren't "creatively billing" prescriptions. If one of the major chains is audited by the very PBM they are a part of, how serious are these audits? As a pharmacist friend of mine says: "It's like the fox guarding the henhouse." Either way you slice it, the PBM company is still making money.

Overall, PBMs are "supposed" to leverage those that are enrolled in their program to negotiate prices with pharmacies (be it retail or mail order) and tackle rebates from the drug manufacturers. The pharmacist has nothing to do with this process. The income train for the PBMs comes from collecting fees from the insurance plan as well as collecting those rebates from the manufacturer. Here is where the smoke and mirrors come on strong. PBMs are NOT required to disclose these discounts they receive. They still sell these drugs at sticker price which is oftentimes way higher than that negotiated price from the manufacturer. You can certainly try to ask for that information however you will be stonewalled due to the idea that this is purely a trade secret. Some states who have grown sick of this lack of transparency have created regulations requiring they know of all discounts and rebates being provided.

I mentioned the term formulary above, but failed to define it. For those of you who don't know what a formulary list is, it is a list of medications that are covered by an insurance. These formularies are usually broken down in to tiers. The tiers typically determine the price. The higher the tier, the higher the price. If a medication is not on that tiered list, it isn't covered. Enter the prior authorization. So, to give you an overview, your doctor meets with you, determines you need medication X, so he/she writes a prescription for you. Your insurance company backed by those fun PBMs dictate whether they will pay. Notice how your health is lost in this. Never mind what medication the doctor determined you need, this is all about what the insurance/PBM think you should have (if anything) instead. Heaven, forbid you need that medication the day it's written because that prior authorization is needed. A prior authorization is basically a "Mother may I" request from the doctor explaining medical necessity to the insurance company why they feel the patient would be best served with taking this medication. In an attempt to get on that formulary, rebates are paid to the PBM by the manufacturer. If there is a rebate, clearly the PBM will pass that savings on to the consumer, right? As you have already guessed, nope. The manufacturer will then point their finger at the PBM stating due to this rebate, they have to raise their prices. PBMs will point their finger at list price increases being the culprit. While they dicker over who is at fault, you are the one who suffers from this pure price gouging.

    This all creates a situation where no one truly knows how convoluted the pricing actually is. Not many can give a straight answer as to how much is truly being saved by the patient. Now would be a great time to ask your local pharmacist, right? How about no? Due to a clause in the PBM contract, the pharmacist cannot proactively tell you that you could save money if you were to pay cash out of pocket or with the infamous drug discount card. In most states, they can only provide that information if the patient asks.

I'm sure you are asking yourself, why would an insurance company/PBM have that much power? What is the overall goal you may ask? The goal is to increase that stock price for their shareholders. Your health means nothing to them. It's a tough pill to swallow……pun intended. Or not, either way, it seemed appropriate.

Chapter Four – Big Pharma

Problems with the system cannot solely be placed upon the PBMs. Big Pharma plays a role as well. For those of you who do not know what that is, let me dive in. Big Pharma is the large conglomeration of the pharmaceutical companies that exert major influence over the economy, our political officials, and our society. I've already touched on the drug pricing in terms of the economic effect in the PBM section. I realize politics are a hot button issue, but just do an internet search on top donors for politicians. This isn't a party thing; this is an across-the-board thing. Drug companies donate millions of dollars to both sides of the aisle. While I have my theories, I ask you: "why would drug companies want to get themselves involved in politics?"

Let's now tackle our impact on society. Let's start with watching TV. During a given hour, I challenge you to count the number of commercials marketing medications. Do you know there are only two countries in the world that allow for direct-to-consumer advertising for prescription medications? Those countries are the United States of America and New Zealand. Why do we need this advertising? It is all about selling you something. Most of them end with the phrase of "ask your doctor about _____." How about let your doctor decide if you need something? But then again, even if they do decide you need something, it may not be covered by your insurance. The loop continues.

Do you think that the advertising stops there? Absolutely not. Enter the drug representative AKA the drug rep. Historically, they would send attractive, scantily clad women or sharp dressed men doused in cologne into doctors' offices handing out pens, staplers, note pads, coffee mugs and multiple other tchotchkes with their drug name plastered all over it. In essence, it would be a bribe given out to sway doctors' prescribing habits. Hell, if I am using your pen, might as well use it to write a prescription for your drug, right? The pharmacy would be the secondary destination for those drug reps. Handouts would continue.

In 2009, the handouts of drug advertising products to the medical community ended. However, the handouts continued in different ways. Those same drug reps will now bring in a sandwich platter, pizza, cookies, etc to the office. They still offer their sales pitch. While the product to sway the prescribing habits of the doctors may have changed, the underlying theme is still there. Help the doctor decide what he/she should prescribe. If you want to find out which drug companies support your local physician, check out the following website:

Dollars for Docs - ProPublica - https://projects.propublica.org/docdollars/

The payments to doctors are broken down into categories such as consulting, food, or lodging. As I just looked at this website, the top doctor earned $29 million in payments. No, that isn't a typo, $29 MILLION!!!!!!! You don't think he is influenced by the drug companies?

Back to your TV commercials. Don't you just love when they start reading the side effects? Sometimes those side effects are just as bad, if not worse than the actual thing they are treating. Here's the kicker, sometimes medications are brought to market to combat the side effects of another medication. How warped is that? I give you the example of proton pump inhibitors. These medications are used for gastroesophageal reflux

AKA heartburn. You know, the heartburn you get from downing fast food on a regular basis? Yes, I know there are other causes, but nutritional deficiencies and mineral imbalances caused by diet play a key role in many disease states. In pharmacy school, most disease states first line of treatment is diet and exercise. Your diet impacts just about everything in your life and with proper diet and exercise, you wouldn't need most medication. So, because the underlying issue isn't addressed, the doctor decides to slap a band-aid on the problem and have you take one of these proton pump inhibitors. The result of taking these on a regular basis is the body's inability to absorb calcium. Calcium is a fundamental element needed in bone health. What happens next? You develop osteoporosis. Don't worry, Big Pharma is here to help. They have a drug for that. Enter the bisphosphonates. They are used to help restore bone density. Do you know the biggest side effect of these medication? GERD – Gastroesophageal Reflux Disease – AKA heartburn. So how do you get off this cycle?

The next stop on the Big Pharma train are the manufacturer discount cards. These are designed as copay assist cards. The drug companies realize their product is too expensive, so what do they do? They offer these cards to those patients with commercial insurance. They will advertise copays as little as $0.00 with a little asterisk next to it. The consumer thinks this medication will now be free!!!

Not so fast. That asterisk references the fine print for you. There you will find the limitations of how much that manufacturer card will really pay. Typically, those cards aren't able to be used by those eligible for federally funded insurance plans, Medicare specifically. So that really works out well for those that may need the medication yet cannot afford it due to their limited income. Do you want to know what the best part is? There are expiration dates on those cards. After about 6-12 months, those cards are now expired. At that time, the consumer will have a few options:

1) Attempt to sign back up and get a new card (if still being offered). This is oftentimes quite the hassle for them.

2) Just deal with it and pay the actual copay now that the discount has fallen off.

3) Talk to their doctor about switching to another medication. However, if you are stabilized on the medication and the doctor doesn't want to mess with that, good luck. Also, if they are bought and paid for by that drug company, do you think there may be a conflict of interest?

Big Pharma has even infiltrated the pharmacies in very insidious ways. Just listen to the advertisements overhead next time to are at the pharmacy. While these are mostly pushing vaccinations, there are others out there trying to get you to buy their products. While we are on the topic of vaccinations, do you know certain drug companies advertise vaccinations on the pharmacy's computer system? The drug company creates a hard stop on payment forcibly making the pharmacy team look at why the vaccination rejected by the insurance. Sure enough, it isn't because the vaccination isn't covered, it is because the drug company wants the pharmacy team to sell you more vaccinations. This is followed up by pharmacy chain middle management checking to make sure their teams are pushing these vaccinations. I was privy to a conference call meeting some time ago where a rep from one of the major drug companies was giving a speech about pushing their new upcoming vaccination. They use the guise of caring for your health, but in the same conference call notes, we were told that for every vaccination we give, we would have to sell 26 prescription medications to equal the amount of money made by a vaccine.

At the end of the day of all of this, we reach the same conclusion that your health is not the priority, but money to be made by Big Pharma is.

Chapter Five – Overprescribing

I already mentioned that in 2022 alone, on average every person in the United States would be getting 15 prescriptions per year. How can that be? Aren't we getting healthier in our society with all the gym memberships and advancements in modern medicine? I reference back to nutritional deficiencies and mineral imbalances. So, what do we do? We run off to the doctor for every sniffle and malady no matter how small. You go there with the expectation that you will get a prescription. If you don't, you feel shortchanged and not cared for properly. If they don't prescribe, their "health grade" may fall which will lead to economic impact for the doctor and practice. But you and I both know; they will prescribe something. Even if that is a vitamin that is available over the counter. It's almost as if doctors get a kick back for every medication they prescribe. Do they? I'll provide some very interesting examples of overprescribing here. The first two are two majorly addictive medications.

    I'll start with opioids. We are all aware of the opioid crisis in the country. While there are illegal drugs being brought in to our country, the pain management clinics are oftentimes to blame as well. I cannot tell you the number of patients headed off to the clinic to get their monthly opioid medications. They call ahead just to make sure we have it. If they are told no, they go off on us about how terrible we are. So, the pain management doctors bring their patients back with no real desire to fix their problem. Their way of fixing the problem is to just keep throwing opioids at them. You have to think. Is it really in their best interest to cure the pain? What happens when they do? Another scary story a former colleague told me about was a phone interaction with a doctor at a local ER. This colleague had a question about a prescription written in the ER. He got in touch with the prescriber who was open enough to state that the hospital told ER doctors to write for small quantities of hydrocodone opioids so that patients would give higher patient satisfaction scores. If patient satisfaction scores were higher, the hospital would get better payments from the government.

    The next example I can provide of a completely overprescribed medication is the amphetamine and amphetamine like medications used to treat ADD and ADHD. It seems today there is almost a badge of honor to be on these medications or to have your children on them. Who remembers what happened when the shortage occurred? I'd have panicking patients or patients' parents calling up the pharmacy and telling me that either they or their child NEEDS the medication and cannot function without it. Is that really the case? What if I were to tell you ADD and ADHD are subjective diagnoses? There is no quantitative number or blood marker to diagnose it. There are assessments you can take. If you feel a certain way, you may answer just to ensure you get the medication. It isn't like a blood pressure reading which at a specific number you are diagnosed with hypertension. What's the result? An overwhelming number of ADHD diagnoses in children and adults alike. While I cannot say if your local pharmacist will tell you which doctors are writing medications loosely, I will bet my three pharmacist licenses they can all name at least one. This information can be brought to the attention of your pharmacy's corporate office, but in the interest of filling prescriptions, they typically turn a blind eye. I experienced an interaction with a patient's mother and stepfather during the shortage. It went like this. Mom starts talking to me about how all four of her children need their ADD medication. I was shocked to think that each and every child of theirs had been diagnosed with it. I explained the shortage and perhaps some ways to get them off it. I gave the example of this. You feed your child cupcakes in the morning and then send them to school. Midway through the morning, they are all hyped up on sugar and won't sit still. In the afternoon, they crash and start to fall asleep. The teacher will then tell the parent what is happening which in turn they will tell the doctor. Next thing you know, diagnosis of ADD/ADHD with amphetamines prescribed. Meanwhile, nutrient deficiencies and improper diet (look up red dye 40) have led to this. After I explained it this way, the step father looked at the mother and said maybe we shouldn't give them cake in the morning. There must be a better way.

I will lastly address the glucagon-like peptide-1 receptor agonists AKA the GLP-1 medications. For those of you who don't know what they are, they are the injectable medications originally written for diabetics which have a side effect of weight loss. This immediately led to doctors prescribing them for weight loss even though not all of them were FDA approved for it. The more people found out about using them for weight loss, the more doctors prescribed them. Again, instead of addressing the underlying issue of diet, people look to the magic bullet. What happens when suppliers cannot keep up the demand? The result were constant backorders. You now had diabetics up against those that were using them for weight loss. Patients would be calling every pharmacy in their area looking for their medication in a panic if they cannot get them. What if the doctor didn't prescribe what they wanted? Down goes that health grade. After all of this, you must think to yourself: if you go to the doctor and don't get a prescription, are you pleased with the visit? I ask again, is this what you think of when you think of healthcare?

Chapter Six – Welcome to the Pharmacy

So, let's go back to our scenario from Chapter One. Your prescription isn't ready. Frustration and questions flood your body. Let's address some of those:

They have 6 people back there; how can it not be ready? The doctor said it would be ready when I go there.

There is so much to unpack here, so let's dive in. Unless you are in a major metropolitan area, the chances of seeing that many employees back there at once is rare. Again, I'm not saying it isn't out there, but chances are a pharmacy that is staffed with 6 technicians is only like that for perhaps an hour or two. That is to say, one shift is ending and another is coming on board. Look at your local pharmacy. How many technicians do you see?

Three, maybe four? Now let's tackle what they need to be doing. One will be running register. One will be running drive thru. One is typing in prescriptions that come in non-stop electronically from doctors. The last one is making "patient care" calls to hit various metric goals. I will table the word **METRIC** for now and do a deep dive on it later. Notice how I have mentioned that NO ONE is actually filling your prescription. Here is the interesting part. This example looks to a pharmacy that is running with four technicians. In most pharmacies, that is a pipe dream. Those jobs that are mentioned above are to be done by perhaps two technicians. You may be asking yourself why? The answer is corporate greed. The pharmacy is

CONSTANTLY being stripped of staff hours. The corporation will state reimbursement rates are poor or we aren't making money, so they think the best way to get that stock price up is to cut staffing. Let's ignore CEOs and the like making millions of dollars. Retail pharmacy corporations would rather cut staff than cut their fat cat bonuses. The next time you go out for your coffee and donut, look at the number of employees ensuring your latte is perfect. Now compare that to the number of technicians working to ensure you don't die from taking the wrong medication. Which one is more important?

In regards to the leftover jobs that aren't being done, enter the pharmacist who has to answer the phone, verify whether the information typed in the computer system is correct, fill the prescription, and ultimately product verify the prescription. In regards to your doctor saying it will be ready when you get there, they are either lying to make you feel good for having you wait hours on end in their office or have absolutely no clue how the entire process works.

The pharmacist is just standing there typing and ignoring me/That pharmacist is just standing there on the phone not doing anything.

Well, the pharmacist is doing more than typing. They are trying to ensure the proper prescription is being given to the proper patient for the proper indication. That is what the whole DUR (drug utilization review) is. Meanwhile, the technicians are asking the pharmacist for their barcode to scan their credentials so that they can continue a transaction at the register, someone is thrusting a product in their face while asking should I take this, they are being asked what aisle the laundry detergent is down, or they are answering the phone for someone who wants to know what time they close even though there is an option for that when calling the pharmacy. Granted, I am giving an overview on the types of interactions, but at the end of the day, there are more and they all happen at one point in time.

All they have to do it slap a label on the box and hand it to me.

This is the equivalent of telling your deli worker, all you have to do it focus on my order and slice my roast beef. I got the idea of the grocery store analogy from the very first pharmacist partner I had once I graduated. He always told me to relate things to the grocery store because most people can relate to that. Just as the deli worker has to put on gloves, open up the package of roast beef, turn the slicer on, and make sure they weight matches what the person requires, the pharmacy staff has steps too. Step number one is typing up your prescription. The information then gets sent electronically to your insurance/PBM. On a good day, they get the green light letting them know the claim is paid. There can be many reasons why a claim would not pay such as refill too soon, days' supply issue (i.e. your insurance will only cover a 30-day prescription and the doctor wrote for 90 days), product not covered by your plan, or your insurance isn't accepted here because your insurance/PBM steers people to their preferred pharmacies. While there are many others, this covers the basics of most issues. You are probably thinking no problem. Well, there is a problem, you failed to realize that other people exist. Your prescription with the multiple issues and steps isn't the only prescription the pharmacy is working on, there are hundreds or more of prescriptions that need this type of attention that are lined up in the pharmacy queue.

This pharmacy is terrible. I wish my insurance would allow me to go to a different one.

I will be the first to admit. There are bad pharmacists and bad technicians. I am not oblivious to this fact; however, I will say most do the job well. What hamstrings them is the multitude of other things thrust on their plate. As it pertains to your insurance and what it requires, well, you always have the option of switching pharmacies, typically for a price.

Speaking of prices, I neglected to mention your professional discount cards you see on TV, in your doctors' offices, in a magazine, or sometimes mailed directly to you. They are designed to give various discounts with all outlandish claims like up to 90% off. Nine times out of ten, you are best served using your insurance, but there are those occasions where the discount card wins. Who doesn't win? The pharmacy team when those various cards are shoved in their faces or thrown on the counter doesn't win. They now play the game of musical discount cards to find the best price. Again, in this economy, I get it. However, please realize that other people exist. The more time you take up in line, the longer other people have to wait. I've even heard an insidious rumor that the PBMs own the discount cards. That way, they can cut down on money being used by the insurance plan and still turn a profit by getting the kickbacks for discount card usage. I have not validated that myself.

Chapter Seven – Metrics, Metrics, and more Metrics

A metric is typically defined as a unit of measurement. So how do metrics come in to play in retail pharmacies? Well, it mostly bounces back to that PBM. Because they have set rules and clauses in their contracts regarding how patients are doing under their rule, oops, I mean their coverage, they have to have a system to measure. Let me get this out of the way right now. Chain pharmacies will state that these metrics are used to measure their teams and their impact on patients and that it has no impact on rating their employees. Some will even say it is only an internal thing and that it means nothing for their teams. That is a bold-faced lie. I've received multiple bonuses over the years for hitting their ever-increasing targets. If you don't get the metric goals the company wants, be prepared to be out of a job quickly. There are a multitude of metrics used by retail pharmacies. I will list and try to explain each.

    1) Answering the phone – no matter the pharmacy, the phone should be answered by

a certain time, typically in 3 rings or less or in 30 seconds. It depends on how the system is arranged.

2) Budget hours – even though you get allotted, say 150 technicians' hours, doesn't mean you should use them all in the eyes of corporate. Store managers may decide that you must use less, or will actually not be forthright enough to tell you how many hours you truly have. So, while the pharmacy manager may fight for more help, they will be stonewalled by a higher up. That pharmacy manager must not fight too hard because they will be deemed insubordinate and creatively fired. See the definition of "quiet firing."

3) Prescriptions filled on time – Every prescription that comes into the pharmacy has a time stamped on it. There is a given amount of time that that prescription must be filled by. If not, the pharmacy gets dinged on this. While each chain has their own percentage target, the underlying theme is the same. Get the prescriptions out as fast as possible or fear the consequences.

4) 90-day prescriptions – The chains want to have more 90-day prescriptions filled instead of 30-day ones. Does your insurance only cover 30 days or can you only afford 30 days? Who cares because the PBMs want to see more 90-day prescriptions filled.

5) Automatic Refills – Pharmacies want to have you signed up for automatic refills so that they can keep you coming back. As an area vice president once told me, if you get people signed up for automatic refills, they won't want to move their prescription. He equated it to have direct deposit at a bank. Yes, you can change it, but it is a hassle.

6) Text messages – The retail pharmacies want your cell phone blown up by text messages so that they can get you to pick up your prescription or refill one even if you don't need it. Believe it or not, there is a metric out there calculating the amount of people signed up for text messaging.

7) Vaccination goals – Flu shot, COVID shot, Shingles, etc all have a quota. This is by no means a book against vaccinations, but I just want to ask how are quotas on shots health care? A supervisor for one of the major chains once told his teams that what we need to do is to tell people the leading cause of liver cancer is Hepatitis B and that we should leverage that information to scare people into getting that vaccine. I ask again, is that health care? Let's also dive in to the flu shot. Flu shots begin to appear in pharmacies mid to late July. As soon as they come into the pharmacy, the team is required to push them. Pharmacies are given weekly quotas

to hit. If they don't hit their "target," managers must get on phone calls asking why. I've been personally told just to bill employees' insurance through the company even if I don't give a shot just to make it look like we've given flu shots. Never mind that being insurance fraud. Never mind July being the middle of summer. Never mind that if you were to get one that early, the immunity wouldn't last the entire flu season. You lose 7-11% immunity every month starting two weeks after getting the shot. If you follow the timeline, when does the flu break out? You see a major uptick from late January through March. Amazingly, pharmacies start to increase their stock of oseltamivir (used to treat the flu) in late September. It's almost as if they know how it is all going to play out by pushing flu shots too soon. Do they? Again, I ask, is this healthcare? Also, in regards to vaccinations, the pharmacy teams are told not to have people make appointments or don't turn anyone away. So, let's recap. The team needs to do all the aforementioned things and now let's throw stopping everything to give a vaccination.

8) Patient care phone calls – Everyday a list of phone calls populates down into the pharmacy for both the pharmacist and technicians to make. These calls can be

anything from refill reminder phone calls to prescription pick up calls. Basically, we are playing big brother making sure you take your medication and ultimately pick it up. The fun in depth phone calls fall here too. Those include disease state management, vaccination calls, missing therapy calls, or social impact calls.

A) Disease state management – this phone call picks a specific medication that you are on. The pharmacist is supposed to talk to you about it, make sure you understand it, and ensure you remain compliant.

B) Vaccination calls – As stated above, patients who are eligible for a certain shot need to be called by the pharmacy team to get them to come in for said shot.

C) Missing Therapy Calls – These are fun. These calls are designed to get you to take more medications. You already see your doctor who believes you need certain therapies. If for some reason, there is a gap in this therapy, your pharmacist is supposed to tell you and with your blessing call your doctor to get it prescribed. I'm not saying your pharmacist isn't qualified to make this call, but there is so much more to it all that we are not privy to. Just by looking at their medication list, we cannot give an adequate answer as to why someone may need more medications. We don't have access to blood work and patient charts. Too bad the PBM wants more.

D) Social Impact calls – Do you have trouble paying bills? Do have trouble making ends meet? Well, your pharmacy team will be calling to ask. How this is in the scope of your pharmacy team is beyond me?!?

Did you notice how medication errors aren't included in all of this as a cause of concern? I'm not saying the corporations don't care, but what I am saying that it is not at the forefront of their concerns. To be blunt, they are a matter of doing business. They are more concerned about putting middle management in place, who oftentimes have no clue about pharmacy, in charge of medical professionals to hit these metric goals in an effort to make the PBMs happy. When I say who have no clue about pharmacy, let me list the backgrounds of the various people I've had in charge of me as a pharmacist. I will let you be the judge as to whether they should have a say in healthcare of pharmacies. There were other pharmacists, people with MBAs, people who worked their way up the corporate ladder from cashier to district management, people from other companies such as designer clothing companies, and grocery store managers. I have worked under many people who have not been to pharmacy school and don't know the first thing about medications or how to run a pharmacy. They create work flow charts putting pharmacists at register just because they can and have the authority to do so. While each one brought their own unique style, I'd argue a good portion had no business in retail pharmacy telling pharmacists what to do and how to treat their patients.

Chapter Eight – Oversight

So, with all this dumping on the pharmacist, there has to be someone out there trying to protect the public. In fact, on paper, there is. They are the state boards of pharmacy. There is a board of pharmacy for each state in charge of rules and regulations. The rules and regulations are set forth in an effort to ensure patients are being cared for safely be it how the pharmacy was initially set up before being officially licensed to creating specific regulations on how they want pharmacies to run in their state. What you will oftentimes see are people sitting on the Board who are employed by the chains. The chains also send planted employees (typically middle management) to the meetings so that if a pharmacist comes out and complains about working conditions, it is documented by the planted employee. How long do you think that complaining employee will still be gainfully employed? In regards to people sitting on the Board who are employed by the chains, how hard do you think they will fight to get more technician hours to help the struggling pharmacy teams? The Boards are about as efficient at protecting pharmacy teams and patients as the government is at using our tax dollars.

Chapter Nine – And In the End

So, what does this all mean for the patient and their interactions in the pharmacy? Well, the metrics all feed back to the PBMs. Your retail pharmacy has to turn around to show that they are the best option for patients to be healthy. They want to take their metric goals to the PBMs and show the data how they are the best at making people compliant and healthy. This in turn earns more contracts for the PBM ultimately increasing their profits. The PBMs need to go away and the system needs to return the ways of old. There is so much more than just slapping a label on it. Do you really think it is in the pharmacy teams' best interest to NOT have your prescription ready for you at a reasonable price? From PBMs getting in the way to unqualified supervisors dictating policy to Boards of Pharmacy being a waste of time and money, gone are the days of the friendly neighborhood pharmacist. Those smiling faces previously mentioned are much different now. Those faces are now stressed and frantic. When your health care is being used as a means to generate profits, you have to begin to ask yourself, do they really want you cured or just healthy enough to make you think it's working and sick

enough to keep coming back?

www.ingramcontent.com/pod-product-compliance
Lightning Source LLC
Chambersburg PA
CBHW071958210526
45479CB00003B/990